Investigate Science

Fun with the Sun

by Melissa Stewart

Content Adviser: Jan Jenner, Ph.D.

Reading Adviser: Rosemary G. Palmer, Ph.D.,
Department of Literacy, College of Education,
Boise State University

COMPASS POINT BOOKS ✦ MINNEAPOLIS, MINNESOTA

Compass Point Books
3109 West 50th St., #115
Minneapolis, MN 55410

Visit Compass Point Books on the Internet at *www.compasspointbooks.com* or e-mail your request
to *custserv@compasspointbooks.com*

Photographs ©: Gregg Andersen, cover (middle), 6, 7, 8, 9, 10, 14, 17, 23, 24 (top); Corbis, cover (back-
ground), 1, 11, 16; PhotoDisc, cover (top right), 1, 4, 19; Mug Shots/Corbis, 5; Jason Lindsey/Dembinsky Photo
Associates, 12; Cheryl A. Ertelt, 13 (top); Rob & Ann Simpson, 13 (bottom); Daniel Hodges, 15 (all); Bill Beatty,
20, 21 (all); Les Tranby, 22, 24 (bottom).

Editor: Christianne C. Jones
Photo Researcher: Svetlana Zhurkina
Designer: The Design Lab
Illustrator: Jeffrey Scherer

Library of Congress Cataloging-in-Publication Data
Stewart, Melissa.
Fun with the sun / by Melissa Stewart.
    p. cm. — (Investigate science)
Includes bibliographical references and index.
Contents: What is a shadow?—From day to night—The reasons for the seasons—Doing more.
ISBN 0-7565-0593-3 (hardcover)
1. Sunshine—Juvenile literature. [1. Sunshine.] I. Title. II. Series.
QC911.2.S74 2004
525'.3—dc22   2003018842

Note to Readers: To learn about the sun, scientists pay close attention to its movements. Then they draw and write about everything they see. Later, they use their drawings and notes to help them remember exactly what they saw.

This book will help you study the sun like a scientist. To get started, you will need to get a notebook and a pencil.

Before you go outside on a sunny day, be sure to apply sunscreen. This will help to prevent you from getting a sunburn. Also, you should never look directly at the sun. It could harm your eyes.

In the Doing More section in the back of the book, you will find step-by-step instructions for more fun science experiments and activities.

In this book, words that are defined in the glossary are in **bold** the first time they appear in the text.

Table of Contents

As you read this book, be on the lookout for these special symbols:

 Read directions *very carefully.*

Ask an adult for help.

Turn to the Doing More section in the back of the book.

What Is a Shadow?

Go outside on a bright, sunny day. Stand with the sun behind you and look at the ground. What do you see? You see your shadow.

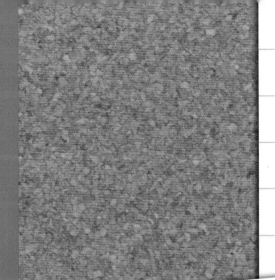

Your shadow follows you everywhere you go. When you run, your shadow runs. When you jump, your shadow jumps. When you stand still, so does your shadow.

Why do you have a shadow? The sun shines on you and around you, but it can't shine through you. Your body blocks the sun's light from hitting the ground. This creates your shadow.

You can also see shadows when you are indoors. When something blocks the light from a lamp or a flashlight, a shadow will appear on the floor or on a wall.

If you stand between a lamp and a wall or shine a flashlight on a wall, you can make shadow puppets. Try moving your hands to make shadows that look like a flying bird, a hopping rabbit, or a scary monster. You can try to create many other shadow puppets as well.

Your hands block the light, which creates a shadow on the wall.

On a sunny morning, grab some colored chalk and go outside. Ask a friend to trace your feet. Then have your friend trace your shadow. Several hours later, stand in the same spot and have your friend trace your shadow again. Draw pictures of both of the shadows in a notebook.

How does your shadow change during the day? When is it longest? When is it shortest? Do you think these changes have anything to do with where the sun is in the sky? Write your findings in the notebook next to the shadow pictures you drew.

Return to the same spot at different times of the day to see how your shadow has changed.

Not all shadows are made by people. Look around you. Objects also make shadows. Trees have shadows, and so do rocks. Even clouds have shadows!

When you walk around your neighborhood, observe things that make shadows. What's the smallest thing you can find that makes a shadow? What's the largest? Look for shadows with strange shapes and draw them.

Go inside and grab a tissue or some toilet paper. Shine a flashlight on it. Does it have a shadow? Compare this shadow to your shadow. Why do you think your shadow is different? Which shadow is darker?

Light can't always travel through an object. Toilet paper is not as thick as your hand, so the light can shine through it.

Even clouds have shadows!

The shadows of these trees have created a shady walking path.

When you are walking outside, watch your shadow closely. It disappears when you walk in shady places. A large object, such as a tree, creates **shade.**

On hot days, dogs and cats often lie in the shade. To find out why, spend 10 minutes sitting quietly in the shade. What do you see, hear, feel, and smell? Make a list of everything you **observe.** Now move into the sun. Sit quietly for 10 minutes, and write down your observations. Why do you think pets like to lie in the shade? Compare your two lists to see what changes from the sun to the shade.

People and animals like to relax in the shade, especially on a warm day.

From Day to Night

During a storm, clouds fill the sky. They block the sun and make a giant shadow. It gets dark outside. It is also dark at night. At night, the sun isn't shining on the place where you live. Hold a soccer ball in front of a lamp, or shine a flashlight on it. Make the room as dark as possible. Does the lamp or flashlight light up the entire ball?

Earth is round like a ball. When the sun lights up one side of Earth, the other side is in the dark. The dark side is in the sun's shadow. It is day where the sun is shining. It is night in the shadow.

When the sun shines on Earth, only part of the planet lights up. To see how this works, shine a flashlight on a soccer ball.

When the sun's light shines on one side of Earth, it is daytime.

When the sun's light is shining on a different part of Earth, it is nighttime.

Sometimes the place you live faces toward the sun.
Sometimes it faces away from the sun. This happens because
Earth is always moving. It spins like a toy top.

Use a globe to see how this works.

Ask an adult to help you find the place
you live. Mark it with a small sticker.
Place the globe in front of a lamp, or
shine a flashlight on it. Now spin the
globe. When the sticker is lit up, it is
day where you live. When the sticker

is in the shadow, it is night.

Did You Know?

Earth makes one full spin every 24 hours.
That's why a day plus a night is 24 hours.

	Sunrise Time	Sunset Time
Sunday	5:03AM	7:18PM
Monday		
Tuesday		
Wednesday		
Thursday		
Friday		
Saturday		
Sunday		
Monday		
Tuesday		
Wednesday		
Thursday		
Friday		
Saturday		

Do you think the sun rises and sets at the same time every day? To find out, write down the time the sun appears and disappears every day for two weeks. You can get the information from a newspaper, the TV news, or on the Internet.

To look at your **data** as a scientist would, make a chart like the one shown here. Compare the times on the first day and the last day. Do you notice any changes over the next two weeks?

The sunrise creates a beautiful glow over the city.

The Reason for the Seasons

Spring

Each **year** has four **seasons**—spring, summer, fall, and winter. Draw a picture of what each season is like where you live. Include plants, animals, the sky, and the ground.

Now compare your pictures like a scientist would. Do the plants look different in each picture? Are the animals doing different things? Do the sky and ground look different? Circle all the things that change with the seasons.

Summer

Fall

Winter

You already know that Earth's spinning causes day and night. As Earth spins, it also travels through space. It makes a giant circle around the sun each year.

Sometimes a toy top tips to one side as it spins. Earth is tipped, too. To see this, look carefully at a globe. It is tilted a little bit. The North Pole is not at the very top of the globe. The South Pole is not at the very bottom.

Earth travels around the sun once each year.

Look closely at a globe to see how it is tilted.

The beam from the flashlight represents the sun's light. When the light shines on the sticker, it is summer where you live.

When you tilt the globe, the sticker moves out of the light. This means it is winter where you live.

Stand about 3 feet (1 meter) from the globe. Tip the globe toward you, and shine a flashlight on the sticker. This is what happens in the summer. The part of Earth you live on is tipped toward the sun. The sun shines directly on the place you live. Direct sunlight makes the days long and hot.

Keep holding the flashlight in the same position. Ask an adult to tip the globe away from you. Where is the flashlight shining now? This is what happens in the winter. Your home is tipped away from the sun. The sun shines directly on the lower half of the world. The days become short and cold where you live.

Now that you know how Earth moves around the sun, you can understand what causes shadows, day and night, and even the four seasons. Keep observing and exploring. There are all kinds of ways to have fun with the sun.

Activity One

On page17 you looked at a globe to understand how Earth's spinning causes day and night. When the place you live faces toward the sun, it is day. When the place you live is turned away from the sun, it is night. To learn more about how Earth's movements affect time of day, try this experiment. Use a flashlight or lamp as your sun.

1. Turn the globe slowly and watch the sticker closely. Notice when the sticker first moves into the light. This is sunrise where you live. It is sunset when the sticker first moves into darkness. Noon is when the sticker is halfway in between the light and dark.

2. Move the globe until it is midnight where you live. When it is midnight where you live, where is it noon? Where is the sun rising and setting?

3. Ask an adult to help you find the following cities on the globe and mark each one with a sticker.

Mexico City, Mexico   Nairobi, Kenya

Rio de Janeiro, Brazil   Dhaka, Bangladesh

Paris, France   Melbourne, Australia

4. When the sun is rising where you live, in which of these cities is it daytime? Where is it night? Is the sun rising or setting in any of the cities you marked?

5. Make a chart like the one below and write down all your observations. You will need to turn the globe so it is noon, sunset, and midnight where you live.

TIME OF DAY . . .

At My House	Sunrise	Noon	Sunset	Midnight
In Mexico City, Mexico		Day		
In Rio de Janeiro, Brazil				
In Paris, France				
In Nairobi, Kenya				
In Dhaka, Bangladesh				Day
In Melbourne, Australia				

Activity Two

On page 25 you learned what causes the seasons. During the summer, the sun shines directly on the place you live. To show that the summer sun really heats things up, try this experiment.

1. Line a bowl with aluminum foil, and fold over the edges.

2. Find a thin stick to put your marshmallow on. Slide a marshmallow onto the stick, and place it in the bowl.

3. Cover the bowl with plastic wrap. Use a rubber band to hold it in place.

4. Put the bowl in a sunny spot, and check it every 15 minutes. How long does it take for the marshmallow to get warm and soft?

5. Compare the taste of a sun-cooked marshmallow to one straight out of the bag. Do they feel the same in your mouth?

6. Try the experiment again at other times of the year. What happens?

Glossary

data information gathered for experiments or projects

globe a round model of Earth that shows oceans and land

observe to use all five senses to gather information about the world

season one of the four time periods that make up a year

shade a shadow made by a large object, such as a tree or building

year the amount of time it takes for Earth to travel once around the sun

To Find Out More

At the Library

Asch, Frank. *The Sun Is My Favorite Star*. San Diego: Harcourt Brace, 2000.

Branley, Franklyn M. *The Sun: Our Nearest Star*. New York: HarperCollins, 2002.

Calvert, Deanna. *Shadows*. New York: Children's Press, 2003.

Pluckrose, Henry Arthur. *Day and Night*. Milwaukee, Wis.: Gareth Stevens, 2001.

Quiri, Patricia Ryan. *Seasons*. Minneapolis: Compass Point Books, 2001.

Places to Visit

Museum of Science

Science Park

Boston, MA 02114

To check out exhibits that explore many different areas of science

On the Web

For more information on the sun and shadows, use FactHound to track down Web sites related to this book.

1. Go to *www.compasspointbooks.com/facthound*
2. Type in this book ID: 0756505933
3. Click on the *Fetch It* button.

Your trusty FactHound will fetch the best Web sites for you!

31

Index

About the Author

Melissa Stewart earned a bachelor's degree in biology from Union College and a master's degree in science and environmental journalism from New York University. After editing children's science books for nearly a decade, she decided to become a full-time writer. She has written more than 50 science books for children and contributed articles to ChemMatters, Instructor, MATH, National Geographic World, Natural New England, Odyssey, Science World, and Wild Outdoor World. She also teaches writing workshops and develops hands-on science programs for schools near her home in Northborough, Massachusetts.